RENOIR
COLOUR & NATURE

BY
DAVID SPENCE

THE ARTIST & HIS TIMES

THE WORLD OF RENOIR

*P*ierre Auguste Renoir was born in Limoges, France, on 25 February 1841. His father, Leonard Renoir, was a tailor; his mother, Marguerite Merlet, a dressmaker. The family moved to the Louvre area of Paris when Pierre was just four years old, making home at 23 Rue d'Argenteuil. Leonard,

Detail showing Renoir's portrait.

Marguerite and their five children shared the Paris apartment which Renoir later recalled as the size of a 'pocket handkerchief'. Leonard continued his business as a tailor from the Rue d'Argenteuil apartment, his tailor's bench being transformed into his own bed at night. Renoir was the second youngest so gradually, as his elder brothers Henri and Victor found jobs and moved out of the family home, the pressure on space eased. The family lived in the very centre of Paris and could observe from their windows the riots of 1848 which led to the

Revolution, which in turn installed Louis Napoleon Bonaparte as President of the Republic of France and then Emperor. Renoir grew up in a city being transformed by revolutions of state, industry and, most, importantly of all, culture.

PORTRAIT OF 43 PAINTERS IN THE STUDIO OF GLEYRE, c.1862

In 1862, at the age of twenty-one, Renoir was accepted at the École des Beaux-Arts to study art. He was an average pupil frustrated as many of the students were by the unadventurous traditional teaching methods with their dependence on studies from models of antiquity. From 1861 Renoir had attended classes in the private studio of the Swiss painter, Charles Gleyre. Many young hopefuls were attracted to Gleyre's style of teaching which was far more liberal than the established schools despite the fact that Gleyre's own painting did not manage to raise itself above the average. Renoir's fellow pupils included Claude Monet, Alfred Sisley and the talented Frédéric Bazille who was tragically to die in the Franco-Prussian war. This group portrait picture of 43 painters in Gleyre's studio includes a portrait of Renoir, painted by his friend Emile-Henri Laporte.

BATHERS IN THE SEINE
(LA GRENOUILLÈRE), 1869

This painting by Renoir is one
of four he made of the subject.
He painted the scene *en plein-air*
(outdoors) on site. Claude Monet
was another painter of the time who
went to La Grenouillère to paint.
Monet described his plans in a letter
to Bazille; *'I have a dream, a picture,
the bathers at La Grenouillère. I have
done some poor sketches for it,
but it is only a dream.
Renoir, who has just
spent two months here,
also wants to paint
this motif.'*

HE ISLAND BAL DE LA GRENOUILLÈRE

The bathing pools at
La Grenouillère, just
20 minutes by train
from the central Paris
station of Saint-Lazare,
were a popular day trip
destination for Parisians
relaxing on weekends or
holidays. Although La
Grenouillère translates as
'frog-pond' the name had
nothing to do with any frogs
that may have lived in the
ponds. 'Frogs' was the name
given by men to the girls who
spent the summers at the pools
and who had a reputation for
being flirtatious. Renoir described
the 'frogs' as being *'very good sorts'*
and found several models who
would pose for him among the
bathers at La Grenouillère.

THE PORCELAIN PAINTER

At the age of thirteen Renoir was apprenticed to a porcelain painter
who decorated vases and plates. His brother, Henri, was already established
as an engraver and Renoir's family encouraged their children in their
artistic trades, eager no doubt to see some money coming in to the
family home. Renoir experimented with decorative painting on
fans and furniture as well as porcelain. This vase, painted by
Renoir when he was an apprentice, is decorated with
figures based on Jean Goujon's *Nymphs*.

INFLUENCES & EARLY WORKS:
ROMANCE & REALISM

PORTRAIT OF ROMAINE LACAUX
(detail), 1864

This portrait of the daughter of a porcelain manufacturer is one of Renoir's earliest commissioned paintings, as well as one of his most accomplished. Painted when he was only twenty-four years old, Renoir has managed to capture the freshness of youth and clear-eyed innocence of the young Romaine.

Renoir's grounding in painting began as a commercial artist painting figures and scenes on porcelain until this craft was made redundant by the introduction of machine printing. This early experience of copying classical figures and rococo scenes helped Renoir acquire skills which he retained all his working life, as well as developing a lasting interest in the work of the classical masters. His early career as a painter, however, began with his studentship under Charles Gleyre, and continued with his admiration of the works of 19th-century French artists Eugène Delacroix and Gustave Courbet. In 1848 Courbet had caused a stir in the art world with his realistic paintings depicting simple everyday scenes, such as road-mending peasants breaking stones. This realism reflected Courbet's view of the world and art's place within it, and was a break from the traditional subjects thought suitable for art, such as scenes from antiquity painted in a formal classical style. Courbet's break with tradition made it possible for artists such as Édouard Manet to concentrate on realistic scenes and began to free artists from the tyranny of tradition.

WOMEN OF ALGIERS

Eugène Delacroix

Delacroix was considered a great artist even in his own time. His painting was very influential during the first half of the 19th century. He was a champion of Romantic art which represented uncontrolled nature, including 'human nature' or actions, as opposed to the tradition of classicism which represented fixed ideas of behaviour and standards of beauty. Romanticism was therefore considered 'modern' and attracted modern-thinking artists. Romantic art sometimes looked towards Oriental subject matter which was considered exotic and exciting.

WOMAN OF ALGIERS *(detail)*

In 1870 Renoir painted this portrait of a woman of Algiers, heavily influenced by the oriental style that was fashionable at the time. It owes much to Delacroix's painting of the same subject but Renoir's painting has made the transition from an imaginary scene to a very real one. Delacroix's paintings were dominated by Romantic notions of exoticism relying on imaginary far away places. Renoir's *Woman of Algiers*, dressed in an exotic and colourful costume, is depicted as a very real woman. The model was actually Renoir's nineteen-year-old girlfriend Lise Trehot who directly engages the viewer's gaze in a very sensual way.

By placing her in an Oriental costume rather than contemporary French dress Renoir does not offend his viewer's idea of how women should behave.

INFLUENCES & EARLY WORKS:
IMPRESSIONISM

*R*enoir's fellow pupils at Charles Gleyre's studio, Monet, Bazille and Sisley, all continued to work together after Gleyre's retirement in 1864. Monet persuaded them to travel to Fontainebleau to paint directly from nature. Renoir's first submission to the official Paris Salon annual exhibition of painting in 1864 was entitled *Esmeralda Dancing with a Goat*. The fact that the picture was accepted tells us a lot about the painting because the work of the Realists and Impressionists were continually rejected by the Salon. No record exists of this painting because Renoir later destroyed it on the grounds that it contained asphalt and would not last, although possibly it was because he was not content with the way it appeared. Renoir and his fellow painters had set about painting the world around them – the Paris street scenes, local bathing spots, boating on the river Seine and scenes from the cafés and music halls. In 1874 the Société Anonyme des Artistes formed to exhibit their pictures, independent from the official Salon, The first exhibition contained works by Monet, Morisot, Renoir Degas, Pissarro, Cézanne, Pissarro and Sisley. The group became known as the Impressionists.

THE POPPY FIELD AT ARGENTEUIL

Claude Monet

This picture was painted by Monet in 1873, the year before the first Impressionist exhibition. It shows two pairs of figures walking through a poppy field near his home at Argenteuil on a warm summer's day and has become one of Impressionism's best-known images. Renoir visited Monet at Argenteuil and they went out into the surrounding countryside to paint. Monet and Renoir shared lodgings together when they were young and poor. Renoir later explained that they spent all their money on studio rent, models and coal for the stove to keep the model warm. They would time their cooking with their painting so the hot stove both warmed the model and cooked the food.

COUNTRY FOOTPATH IN THE SUMMER, 1874

This picture of figures walking along a country footpath painted in 1874 is full of the sunlight which filled Monet's landscapes. The scene is remarkably similar to Monet's painting of the Argenteuil poppy fields and shows Renoir as a true adherent to Impressionist painting at that time. When the Impressionists mounted their second exhibition in 1876 at Durand-Ruel's gallery in the Rue le Peletier, Renoir was represented by 15 pictures. Although Impressionism still had its critics Renoir managed to sell six pictures and was finding admirers such as the publisher Georges Charpentier who commissioned Renoir to paint a family portrait. This relative success enabled Renoir to rent a house and gave him a degree of stability which allowed him to concentrate on his art.

LISE *(detail)*, 1868

Renoir had some early successes with paintings being accepted by the official Salon in the 1860s, such as this portrait of Lise. This painting of girlfriend Lise Trehot was unusual in that it was full length, a convention normally reserved for royalty.

Artist and critic Zacharie Astruc described Lise as '*the daughter of the people, with all her typical Parisian features*'.

One reaction to the picture was; '*The whole thing is so natural and has been observed so accurately that it will appear wrong…we are used to imagining nature in terms of conventional colours.*'

The painting was purchased by the writer Theodore Duret for 1,200 francs.

THE ART OF HIS DAY

Renoir's career as a painter developed alongside the Impressionists who are so well known today. Their depictions of comfortable middle class scenes either in the Parisian streets or surrounding countryside differed from the earlier Realist imagery such as Millet's peasant scenes, but nevertheless sought to paint pictures of real life as they experienced it. Many of Renoir's contemporaries, however, continued to paint in the traditional way, depicting religious or mythological scenes in a highly finished style. These artists found continued acceptance at the official Salon where their paintings were exhibited. The Impressionist's paintings with their sketchy unfinished style and modern subject matter were considered too shocking to be exhibited at the Salon where the unsuspecting French public might see them. The technology of the day also had an impact on the development of Impressionism. The growing number of newspapers and journals circulated wider and wider thanks to more efficient and cheaper reproduction methods, and an increasingly literate public were able to read about the latest art, and see reproductions. The movement even owed its name to a journalism. A review by critic Louis Léroy referred to the 'Exhibition of Impressionists' in the magazine *Le Charivari*.

THE GULF OF MARSEILLES

Paul Cézanne

Paul Cézanne was the son of a hat-maker who moved into banking and became a wealthy citizen of his home town of Aix-en-Provence. Cézanne studied art in Paris where he met Pissarro and the circle of Impressionist painters with whom he exhibited in 1874. He met and fell in love with artist's model Hortense Fiquet in Paris and they had an illegitimate son whose existence Cézanne kept from his parents. When they discovered the truth they halved his allowance leaving the family to borrow money where they could. When Cézanne inherited his father's fortune he concentrated on painting in Provence, concerning himself with form and space, making 'something solid' of Impressionism.

LE PONT DE L'EUROPE

Gustave Caillebotte

Gustave Caillebotte was a wealthy collector of Impressionist paintings and a talented artist in his own right. His work was not considered to be as important as the Impressionists but in the 1960s his art was 'rediscovered' and is now very popular. Caillebotte painted domestic everyday scenes of Paris life using dramatic perspective and a more highly finished technique than his Impressionist friends. There is an overwhelming sense of modernism in his paintings, stressed by the open air 'snapshot' feeling as if the image has been captured through the lens of a camera. His paintings were respected by his friends and contemporaries and were exhibited at the Impressionist exhibition of 1876. Caillebotte built up a large collection of Impressionist paintings including ten by Renoir, often buying them from friends at inflated prices in order to support them. In his will he left his collection to the State on the condition that they be exhibited at the Louvre. When he died in 1894 the more conservative artists protested that if the State accepted his collection it would be a sign of moral decline and the end of the nation. Eventually 38 of the 57 paintings were exhibited, supposedly on the grounds of a lack of space at the Louvre.

THE LIFE OF RENOIR

~1841~
Born on 25 February
at Limoges, France

~1844~
Renoir family move to Paris

~1854~
Renoir becomes an
apprentice at Levy Brothers,
painting plates and vases

~1858~
Made redundant by new
technique for printing
onto porcelain

~1862~
Studies at Charles
Gleyre's studio
where he meets
Sisley, Monet
and Bazille

PORTRAIT OF JULIE MANET

Berthe Morisot

Berthe Morisot's truly Impressionist paintings of elegant Parisian women are notable for their freshness and delicacy. Morisot was able to paint the crisp starched linen and soft silk of evening dress with blurred brushstrokes which are dragged across the surface of the canvas retaining their immediacy of touch. The 'impression' of having captured the fleeting moment as a woman prepares to dress for the evening or, interrupted, glimpses towards the viewer, makes her a true Impressionist. Morisot married Édouard Manet's brother, Eugene, and they had a daughter, Julie, who appears in a number of the Impressionist group's paintings including those by Renoir.

THE LIFE OF RENOIR

~1864~
Has a painting accepted by the Salon but later destroys it

~1865~
Meets Lise Trehot who becomes his girlfriend and model

~1872~
Has two paintings purchased by dealer Durand-Ruel and spends the summer painting with Monet

~1874~
Exhibits at the first Impressionist show

~1880~
Meets Aline Charigot

~1881~
Travels to Algeria, Venice, Rome and Naples

~1883~
Experiments with new 'Dry Style' of painting

~1885~
Birth of his son Pierre

~1888~
First attack of rheumatoid arthritis which leaves his face partially paralysed

~1892~
Young Girls at the Piano purchased by the State

~1894~
Birth of son Jean

~1890~
Marries Aline Charigot

~1901~
Birth of son Claude (Coco)

GABRIELLE ET JEAN *(detail)*, C.1895

Renoir's second son, Jean, was born on 15 September 1894. In Jean Renoir's own memoirs of his father he writes that his mother exclaimed on his birth; *'Heavens how ugly, take it away!'* Jean became a famous film director as well as a writer of several books, including a biography of his father. Another witness to Jean's birth was Gabrielle Renard, the fifteen-year-old cousin of Aline Charigot who had come from her home in Essoyes to help with the preparations for the birth. Gabrielle stayed to help look after Jean. She became Renoir's favourite model, at first posing with the children such as in this portrait with Jean, but in Renoir's later years she became an important figure in Renoir's exploration of the female form in such paintings as *Gabrielle with Jewel Box* (page 24). Gabrielle continued as Renoir's principal model until 1914 when she married and left the Renoir home in Cagnes.

THE CLOWN
(detail), 1909

Claude Renoir was born in 1901 when Renoir was sixty years old. Claude was only fourteen when his mother, Aline, died at the age of fifty-six, after fighting diabetes. Claude, nicknamed Coco, was often a model for Renoir and in this painting the six-year-old Claude is dressed in a clown's outfit.

DÉJEUNER A BERNEVAL, C.1905

This is a charming domestic interior scene, at home with the Renoir family.

FAMILY, FRIENDS & OTHERS

Renoir did not come from a comfortable middle class family as did many of his Impressionist friends. His father's tailoring business was just sufficient to support the family and Renoir found a job as an apprentice to a porcelain painter when he was thirteen to supplement the family income. When he decided to study painting at the studio of Charles Gleyre he soon became friends with Claude Monet, Frédéric Bazille and Alfred Sisley. He kept company with this artistic circle and had many girlfriends among the models who posed for his paintings, but it was not until Renoir was nearly forty that he met Aline Charigot, a nineteen-year-old dressmaker who lived nearby Renoir's home in the Rue Saint-Georges.

Aline posed for Renoir and fell in love with him despite her mother's advice to find a man who was old and wealthy. Aline travelled to Italy with Renoir in 1881 and much later referred to the trip as their 'honeymoon', despite the fact they were not actually married until 1890.

BUST OF MADAME
RENOIR WITH PIERRE

Aline Charigot came from the Burgundy area of France and was teased by her Parisian friends about her accent and country ways. When they first met, Renoir and Aline spent much of their time together by the river Seine, travelling by train from Saint-Lazare to the Chatou bridge and then the Fournaise restaurant. Renoir's well known painting *Luncheon of the Boating Party* (page 17) depicts a scene at the Fournaise restaurant which shows Aline holding a small dog. Aline moved in with Renoir after his return from a trip to Algeria in 1881. Their first child, Pierre, was born in 1885. Renoir found a studio near the family apartments in the Rue Houdon in order that, according to Aline, '*the baby will be able to cry to his heart's content.*' Pierre became an actor but went to fight in the First World War were he was badly wounded.

FAMILY, FRIENDS & OTHERS

The small group of friends who studied together under Charles Gleyre and then continued to paint together were at the very centre of the movement which was subsequently named Impressionism. In 1865 Renoir shared a studio with Alfred Sisley and a year later, after Sisley was married, he moved in with Frédéric Bazille, a talented young painter who was tragically killed at the age of twenty-nine during the Franco-Prussian war.

In 1867 Bazille rented a Paris studio at 20 rue Visconti. From here he wrote to his mother; *'Since my last letter there is something new at the rue Visconti. Monet has fallen from the sky with a collection of huge canvases which will be a great success at the World Fair. He will stay here until the end of the month. With Renoir that makes two needy painters that I'm housing. It's a veritable sanatorium. I'm delighted, I have plenty of space, and both are very good company.'* Renoir and Bazille continued to be close friends, later moving together to a studio near the famous Café Guerbois which became the meeting place for the new wave of modern-thinking artists such as Manet, Monet, Degas, and Pissarro, as well as writers like Émile Zola, Edmond Duranty and Zacharie Astruc.

PORTRAIT OF JULIE MANET (detail), c.1894

Julie Manet often stayed with the Renoir family, particularly after the death of her parents, Berthe Morisot and Eugène Manet, which left her orphaned at the age of seventeen. Morisot had asked Renoir to look after Julie although her official guardian was the poet Stéphane Mallarmé.

MADAME ALPHONSE DAUDET (detail), 1875

Alphonse Daudet was a successful novelist and playwright who was r[...] as one of the leading members of the Realist movement in literature together with writers such as Émile Zola. Daudet was a great supporter of Impressionism, commissioning this portrait of his wife and buying works from a number of other artists. Daudet was a frequent visitor to the Nouvelle-Athènes café, mixing with the artistic set who met to talk about their work. He was also often invited to Renoir's house where he would join the likes of Zola, Odilon Redon and Stéphane Mallarmé for dinner.

PORTRAIT OF CLAUDE MONET (detail), 1875

Claude Monet moved to Argenteuil, a suburb of Paris, in 1871. Renoir was amongst the many visitors that stayed with Monet at Argenteuil. When they were together Monet persuaded Renoir to take up his easel and go out into the countryside to paint, *en plein-air*. Several of Renoir's paintings are of views of the Seine such as the picture of racing boats entitled *The Seine at Argenteuil*. Renoir also made numerous portraits of his friend Claude Monet and Claude's wife Camille. Monet's obsession with capturing in paint the changing moods of his subject matter according to the light made him the leading exponent of Impressionism. In his own words, Monet wanted to *'ensnare the light, and throw it directly on to the canvas'*.

PORTRAIT OF RICHARD WAGNER, 1882

Renoir was introduced to Wagner's music by a friend at a time when national sentiment was against the composer. This made Renoir determined to like his music and Renoir was eventually introduced to Wagner in person, at which time he made three sketches, (executed in under an hour) and this portrait. During the meeting Wagner managed to offend the artist because of his views of French composers whom Wagner hated. Renoir expressed his like for the music of Offenbach which Wagner dismissed as *'little music, but not bad'*. Later on Renoir attended a performance of Wagner's opéra *Die Walküre* at Bayreuth, and commented; *'They have no right to shut people up in the dark for three solid hours…you are forced to look at the only place where there is any light; the stage. It's absolute tyranny…We might as well be frank about it; Wagner's music is boring.'*

LE MOULIN DE LA GALETTE, 1876

The painting, which has been described as the most beautiful picture of the 19th century, appears at first glance to be chaotic. The foreground and background merge and the overlapping forms of the figures are often indistinguishable. The sunlight that filters through the foliage casts shadows that fall across the figures and ground alike, creating a dappled effect that unifies the picture.

Renoir made many studies from models for his figures in *Le Moulin de la Galette*. The two young girls in the centre of the picture, one resting her arm on the other's shoulder, are Jeanne and Estelle, seamstresses known as 'grisettes,' dressed in the latest Paris style. Renoir described how he saw Jeanne on the streets of Montmartre, thought her the ideal model, and stopped and spoke to her. *'I don't go in for that sort of thing Monsieur,'* she replied. Renoir noted that; *'She had lovely hands, the ends of her fingers were swollen from being pricked by needles.'* Eventually Renoir persuaded Jeanne's mother to let her daughter pose for him in return for payment, and soon Jeanne's sister Estelle also became Renoir's model.

The pair of dancers depicted centre-left is the Cuban painter Pedro Vidal with Margot Legrand. Margot appears to be the same young girl who Jean Renoir recalls was nursed by his father and Dr Gachet, but she died of suspected small-pox three years after this picture was painted.

WHAT DO THE PAINTINGS SAY?

PARIS SOCIETY

The years before the end of the 19th century are known in France as the Belle Époque, the golden age when life was for the enjoying. This description does not convey the fact that it was also the time when many were struggling for equal rights such as workers and women in general. Nevertheless it was a time when Paris prospered with new roads, railways and buildings and the middle classes became more secure and prosperous. Mass entertainment was available in the form of the café-concerts and dance halls, the most popular of which was the *Folies-Bergère* which still exists today. Renoir painted modern Parisian life. Images of young people at play, in the park, the dance hall, strolling along the boulevards show us the pleasant side of Paris life. Renoir was aware that he concentrated on the nice things when he said *'There are enough unpleasant things in this world. We don't have to paint them as well.'* Although Renoir concentrated on the pleasant side of life he painted scenes from the ordinary everyday world of the Parisian worker at play, not the fashionable well-to-do classes, and it is this record of real life that makes his painting fascinating.

The pipe smoker (on the right) is Norbert Goeneutte and seated next to him with pen poised is writer Georges Rivière.

DANCING AT THE MOULIN DE LA GALETTE

A building programme in the 1860s and 1870s transformed the landscape of Paris. Some of the surrounding parishes became part of the city as it grew and grew. Montmartre had been a village on a hill with windmills and vineyards, before it was swallowed-up by Paris. The fashion for public dances in the 1870s meant that nearly every available space in Paris, from bars and courtyards to squares and parks, were at some time used for this new craze. The best-known dance-bar in Montmartre was le Moulin de la Galette, or 'le Radet' for short. It had an outdoor dance floor as well as a bar for red wine and 'galettes', a kind of circular waffle from which it gained its name.

THE ARTIST'S VISION

FAMOUS IMAGES

By the end of the 1870s Renoir was no longer exhibiting with the Impressionists and had decided to follow his own individual course. When he painted the *Luncheon of the Boating Party* in 1881 he had already made a break with Impressionism. He stated that *'I had wrung Impressionism dry, and I finally came to the conclusion that I neither knew how to paint nor draw. In a word, Impressionism was a blind alley.'* His tours of Algeria and then Italy gave him new inspiration and new direction, and he re-discovered the works of the Old Masters. The style employed in the execution of the *Luncheon of the Boating Party* is more assured than that of *Le Moulin de la Galette* painted five years earlier. The individual figures portrayed are more clearly defined, particularly by the use of stronger colour, and the forms appear to be gaining greater form and solidity.

YOUNG WOMAN WITH A FAN (*detail*), 1881

This portrait of Alphonsine, daughter of restaurant owner Alphonse Fournaise, captures the charm which made her a favoured model with many male admirers. She features in *Luncheon of the Boating Party*, leaning against the rail.

THE LUNCHEON OF THE BOATING PARTY, 1880/1

The scene depicted in this well-known painting is the Restaurant Fournaise on the Ile de Chatou, a little island in the river Seine near the Ile de Croissy. It was a short train ride from Renoir's studio in the centre of Paris. The owner of the restaurant, Alphonse Fournaise, had built a landing stage for the Parisians who wished to swim and hire boats on the river, and he began to serve refreshments on the stage. Renoir recalls the place *'where life was a perpetual holiday and the world knew how to laugh in those days.'* Renoir often used to visit the Restaurant Fournaise with his girlfriend Aline.

The figure wearing a top hat and engaged in conversation at the back of the scene is the banker and art collector Charles Ephrussi.

Aline Charigot, Renoir's future wife, sits at the table holding a small dog. Behind is Alphonse Fournaise, the restaurant owner.

RENOIR'S FRIENDS

In the background is Paul Lhote holding actress Jeanne Samary by the waist.

The seated figure wearing the straw hat is painter Gustave Caillebotte who talks to actress Ellen Andrée.

The painting shows many of Renoir's friends, several of whom sat for Renoir in his studio so he could finish the picture. The group is notable for its social mix, with flower sellers and bankers drinking side by side. The relaxed scene is full of meaningful glances and intimate touches. The arrangement of figures around a table laden with fruit and wine suggests there is more to the picture than simply a group portrait of Renoir's acquaintances.

THE UMBRELLAS, 1881/5

This painting clearly demonstrates Renoir's different approaches to painting in the 1880s. The artist returned to this painting again and again over a period of years. The figures on the right of the picture are painted in Renoir's 'Impressionist' style of the 1870s with bright colours but soft outlines and looser brushstrokes. The two figures on the left however were painted in a later style which has more clearly defined outlines, a more 'finished' surface and more subdued colours.

It is thought that the painting was begun around 1881 because the right-hand figures are wearing dresses and hats that were fashionable at that time, and Renoir normally dressed his models in the latest fashions. By 1883 simpler dresses came into style and the woman holding a basket is dressed in a style which was the height of fashion in 1885, but which had fallen out of fashion by 1887. Recent X-ray examination of the painting suggests that the woman on the left was first painted in the earlier Impressionist method around 1881 with skirts similar to the other women in the picture, complete with white lace cuffs and collar and a hat. This figure was over-painted in about 1885.

DETECTION THROUGH COLOUR

Further examination of *The Umbellas* reveals the presence of cobalt blue pigment in the right hand section of the picture and in the original painting underneath the left-hand figures. This pigment was used by Renoir only during the 1870s and early 1880s. French Ultramarine, a pigment used later by Renoir, was found in the colours on the left-hand figures we see today. He also experimented with removing the oil medium and replacing it with a water-based medium to bind the colours because he thought the oil would eventually darken and spoil his colours, although this experiment was without success. This examination of the use of pigments and medium enables art historians to find out the history of the painting.

HOW WERE THEY MADE?
THE DRY STYLE

*W*hen Renoir visited Italy in 1881 he went to see the art of the great masters such as Michelangelo, Raphael and Bernini. He later recalled that he became tired of the draped figures with too many folds and muscles, and preferred the Pompeiian frescoes in the Naples Museum. He marvelled at the wonderful colours achieved by the fresco painters with such a limited range of colours made from earths and vegetable dyes, and even confessed to repairing a wall painting using paints in powder form that he found in a nearby mason's house. The experience of Renoir's Italian trip was certainly one factor that made him change the way he was painting. By 1883 Renoir openly admitted that Impressionism was a dead end and that he was looking for a new style. He rejected the Impressionist way of painting outdoors, stating that *'An artist who paints straight from nature is really only looking for nothing but momentary effects. He does not try to be creative himself, and as a result the pictures soon become monotonous.'* Renoir's exploration of new ways of painting in the 1880s have now become known as his 'Dry Period'.

THE SCHOOL OF ATHENS *(detail)*

Raphael

Renoir's gradual disillusionment with the Impressionist style of rapidly building-up the surface of the canvas with touches of colour was hastened by what he saw on his trip to Italy. He admired the purity and grandeur of Raphael's wall-paintings which retained bright colourful surfaces and were masterful compositions with great clarity of structure and form.

WHAT DO THE PAINTINGS SAY?
A NEW DIRECTION

Renoir's 'Dry Period' is also sometimes known as his 'Ingresque' period after the famous French painter Jean Ingres. Ingres was a dominant influence in French painting in the earlier part of the 19th century. Ingres spent a good part of his career in Italy and was a devoted follower of the art of Raphael, the great Italian painter of the High Renaissance. The art of Ingres, in his admiration of Raphael, was in turn admired by Renoir. This direct line of influence extends back to Raphael's source of inspiration; the great classical art of ancient Greece. In pursuing this new direction in his painting Renoir was rejecting the modern art of Impressionism which he felt had lost its way. He was returning to the traditional values which had remained unchanged for centuries. Renoir became interested in the methods of Renaissance artists and he criticized the modern teaching methods which had replaced the apprenticeship system. The culmination of his new direction was a large painting called *The Bathers*.

THE BLONDE BATHER

This painting was made by Renoir in 1887 at the height of his 'Dry Period'. The influence of Ingres is quite evident, the formal pose of the figure against a classical landscape recalling the fresco paintings Renoir had visited during his trip to Italy. The painting resembles fresco painting because of its bright colouring, smooth finish and clear edges around the female form. However Renoir does not resist breaking-up the landscape with individually applied brushstrokes. About this time a critic asked Renoir whether he considered himself a descendant of Ingres, to which Renoir replied *'I only wish I was.'*

BATHER IN A LANDSCAPE – EURYDICE (detail), c.1888

In this painting Renoir not only shows the female figure against an imaginary scene where women in classical Greek dress bathe in the river, but even gives the sitter a name from the mythology of antiquity. Eurydice was the wife of Orpheus and appeared in sculptures from the 5th century BC.

BAIGNEUSE VALPINÇON (detail)

Jean Ingres

The unrivalled draughtsmanship of Ingres inspired many artists, most of whom only managed a poor imitation of Ingres's cool classical expression of form. Some Impressionist painters, particularly Edgar Degas, were influenced by the classical approach to the human form which was at odds with the Romantic movement of the 19th century and which gave rise to Realism, the precursor of Impressionism. Many of Ingres's paintings were based on imaginary Oriental scenes which provided an excus to paint sensuous female nudes.

STUDY FOR THE BATHERS, 1883/5

Renoir began working towards the creation of a large painting of women bathing with a series of drawings and studies. This was a change in working methods for the artist and a clear move towards traditional studio-based ways of painting and therefore further away from Impressionism. The women depicted by Renoir are no longer the modern women of Paris but timeless beauties removed from their real setting and placed in some Eden-like landscape in a golden age full of innocence.

THE BATHERS

Renoir exhibited his new paintings at the Georges Petit Gallery. They were exhibited alongside paintings by artists such as Monet, Pissarro, Morisot and Whistler, and caused something of a stir because of Renoir's departure from Impressionism. The painter Camille Pissarro, a friend of Renoir, wrote to his son; *'Durand has been to Petits; he has seen the Renoirs, and doesn't like his new style – he doesn't like it at all.'* Durand-Ruel was an influential dealer who had championed Impressionist art and he was evidently discouraged to find that one of his artists had now adopted a different style of painting. Pissarro commented on Renoir's new style; *'I can quite understand the effort he is making. It is a very good thing not to want to go on repeating oneself, but he has concentrated all his effort on line. The figures stand out against each other without any sort of relationship and the whole thing is meaningless. Renoir is no draughtsman and without the lovely colours he used to use he is incoherent.'*

**THE GREAT BATHERS –
THE NYMPHS** *(detail)*

Renoir continued the theme of Bathers from the 1880s to the end of his life. This picture was painted about 1918, when Renoir was seventy-seven years old. The figures in the pastoral landscape appear almost to be part of the ground upon which they lie. They have a massiveness and solidity which makes them appear like sculptures modelled out of clay, but are painted in striking flesh tones which are echoed in the grass and the trees which surround them. Renoir was racked by arthritis towards the end of his life and was only able to paint by having his paintbrushes wedged into his bandaged hands. It was in this way that the *Great Bathers* was painted.

NYMPHS BATHING *François Girardon*

This bas-relief of nymphs bathing by the 17h-century artist François Girardon decorates one of the fountain pools in the park of Versailles. Renoir found it a source of inspiration for his *Bathers* picture as well as other works.

THE BATHERS

This painting was made over a period of several years and finally exhibited at Georges Petit's gallery in 1887. Renoir has created a picture which is completely unlike his former Impressionist works. The subject matter is drawn from a classical source and has none of the spontaneity in execution that typifies Impressionism. In fact the pigment was spread with a knife and smoothed over as much as possible to create a highly finished surface. The idealized beauty of the female forms in their carefully arranged poses have nothing to do with Paris in the 1880s and are divorced from any real or natural context. The women recall the porcelain decorations that Renoir made in his youth and the only real similarity with his earlier painting is the richness of colour, particularly in the surrounding landscape, which typifies Renoir's art.

DIANA BATHING

François Boucher

The Rococo style of the 18th century artist François Boucher was much admired by Renoir. Boucher's paintings of beautiful young women in classical landscapes were an obvious inspiration, as much for the subject matter as the style of painting.

GABRIELLE WITH JEWEL BOX, 1911

This painting made in 1910 shows Renoir's late style. The model is Gabrielle Renard, the young cousin of Renoir's wife Aline. Renoir was quite open about his fascination for women's bodies and talked about them in a way some would find unacceptable today. To the artist they were objects to be observed and depicted: the quality of the skin compared to a fruit which must respond well to the light; the arrangement of the facial features must be in harmony *'with almond shaped eyes which should be half-way between the top of the head and the tip of the chin.'* Some critics think that this is why his models appear to be without spirit – they are painted as if they were fruit or flowers. Renoir's depiction of the female form is without lust. The women appear trance-like, increasingly detached from their surroundings.

BATHER WITH LONG HAIR
(*detail*), 1910

Renoir concentrated on voluptuous nudes who posed in a sea of vibrant colour, and it is almost as if his struggle with arthritis which gave him difficulty holding his paintbrushes allowed him the artistic freedom to relax his style, painting in a freer way with looser, broader brushstrokes. The female figures are as one with the landscape, and no longer appear to be conscious compositions, carefully arranged, but merge effortlessly with the background creating natural and sensuous imagery.

THE ARTIST'S VISION

HOW WERE THEY MADE?

THE LATE STYLE

In the 1890s Impressionist painting was becoming established in some circles, particularly with some influential collectors, but as a style of painting it was being surpassed by new styles such as the Symbolism of Paul Gauguin. Renoir by this time was an old man who suffered severe attacks of rheumatoid arthritis which crippled him and forced him to spend the winter months in the relative warmth of the South of France. Finally in 1905 he moved with his family to Cagnes, a small town near Antibes on the Mediterranean coast. He had a house built which he called 'Les Collettes' which was to become his studio until his death. Towards the end of his life his arthritis was so severe that he was permanently wheelchair-bound and his hands became deformed to such an extent that he was unable to hold any object. He continued to paint with brushes wedged into his bandaged hands, and his pictures became more colourful then ever before.

THE JUDGEMENT OF PARIS

Peter Paul Rubens

Renoir's depiction of the female form developed and became more massive, taking on proportions which remind us of the 17th-century Dutch artist Rubens, and dominate the picture frame. The figures are completely timeless and might be from classical mythology or from the present day, but are isolated from everything except their landscape. The backgrounds are reduced to a field of colour, still Impressionistic in execution, and the whole is soaked in the Mediterranean sunlight which make the colours come alive.

CATHERINE HESSLING IN THE FILM NANA (*right*)

Catherine Hessling (also shown with Renoir in his studio) was a model who worked at the Nice Academie de Peinture and who went to work for Renoir when he was looking for models for his large *Great Bathers* painting. Dédée, as she was then known, travelled by train every day from Nice to Renoir's studio in Cagnes to pose for the artist. After Renoir's death in 1919 his son, Jean, married Dédée and she became an actress appearing in the early films directed by Jean Renoir under her stage name Catherine Hessling.

THE AUDIENCE FOR THE PICTURES

*R*enoir had no means of financial support except from odd jobs or from the sale of his paintings. At the beginning of his career as an artist, times were hard. The society formed by the Impressionist group in 1873, with Renoir a member, had to be dissolved in 1875 due to large debts and the artists were forced to sell their pictures. They were auctioned at the Hotel Drouot in Paris on 24 March 1875 with disastrous results. With a hostile crowd and few buyers, Renoir sold twenty canvases for 2,000 francs compared to the 200,000 francs a respected Salon artist could earn for one painting alone. Early on Renoir depended on friends to purchase paintings, receiving support from Édouard Manet, Victor Chocquet and others. Chocquet was a civil servant in the Ministry of Finance who could ill afford to buy paintings. Renoir is reported to have said of him; *'What a charming crackpot...he scraped up the means to buy paintings from his salary...and never gave a thought to whether or not the art would appreciate in value.'*

PORTRAIT OF
DELPHINE LEGRAND *(detail)*, 1878

Some of the most charming of all Renoir's work are his portraits of children. In this picture of Delphine Legrand, daughter of friend and art dealer Alphonse Legrand, Renoir is able to create a sense of innocence and vulnerability which captures the spirit of the sitter.

MONSIEUR AND MADAME BERNHEIM, 1910

The Bernheim family were art dealers who actively supported the Impressionist painters. The Bernheims organised an important exhibition for Renoir in 1900 and continued to represent his work up to and beyond Renoir's death. During this time Renoir made several portraits of the Bernheim family members including this picture of Berheim-Jeune and his wife. The family was very rich, with a magnificent chateau, a house in Paris, a dozen motorcars, and even a dirigible balloon. Most importantly to Renoir, however, was that they had '*beautiful wives whose skins took to the light.*'

MADAME CHARPENTIER *(detail)*

In 1876 Renoir painted this portrait of Marguerite Charpentier, wife of Georges Charpentier, the publisher of famous novelists such as Flaubert, Zola and Maupassant. The family were very wealthy and had a reputation for gathering together the most interesting people of the day; writers, painters, composers, as well as actresses and popular singers. The Charpentiers supported Renoir as they did other artists, commissioning portraits of the family and using their influence to ensure his paintings were exhibited, thereby giving Renoir a degree of financial security. Renoir noted of the sessions with Marguerite Charpentier; '*She reminds me of the sweethearts of my youth, the models of Fragonard. The two daughters had lovely dimples. I was congratulated. I forgot the attacks of the newspapers. I had models who were willing to sit for free and who were full of goodwill.*'

PINK AND BLUE, 1881

Alice and Elizabeth Cahen d'Anvers were daughters of a wealthy banker. Renoir was commissioned to paint several portraits of the two girls after Charles Ephrussi, owner of the *Gazette des Beaux-Arts* had introduced Renoir to the Cahen family. It appears that the Cahens were disappointed with the double portrait and decided to hang it in the servants quarters, out of view of their friends.

NUDE IN THE SUNLIGHT, 1876

In 1876 Durand-Ruel exhibited Renoir's paintings at the Rue le Pelletier, including *Nude in the Sunlight*. The art critic Albert Wolff wrote in *Le Figaro*; *'Try and explain to Monsieur Renoir that a woman's torso is not a mass of rotting flesh, with violet-toned green spots all over it, indicating a corpse in the final stages of decay... And this collection of vulgarities has been exhibited in public without a thought for possible fatal consequences. Only yesterday a poor man was arrested in the Rue le Pelletier, after leaving the exhibition, because he began biting everyone in sight.'*

WHAT THE CRITICS SAY

Renoir's art has justifiably taken its place among the great Impressionist works and he is considered today to be one of the small group who changed the course of art in the latter half of the 19th century. Like his contemporary painters he found acceptance slow during his working life, but towards the end of his career gained recognition, fame and the money that came with it. Renoir never had any pretensions about his art. He wanted to paint what he found attractive and amusing, and by his own admission did not dwell on any concern to express great ideas or emotions. He hated any notion of artists being more than simple labourers who day after day had a job to do – paint. This may be because of his relatively humble beginnings, but whatever the reason critics and especially art historians in the 20th century have regarded his art as somehow slighter, less important than his contemporaries. By contrast the non-specialist public at large have always found his art attractive, accessible and enjoyable.

PORTRAIT OF A YOUNG GIRL *(detail)*, 1888

Renoir's habit of making the eyes of his portrait subjects dark in contrast to the surrounding pale face attracted the attention of Arthur Baignieres, who wrote of Renoir's painting *Mother and Children* in 1874; *'From afar we see a bluish haze, from which six chocolate drops forcefully emerge. Whatever could it be? We come closer; the sweets are the eyes of three people and the haze a mother and her daughters.'*

YOUNG GIRLS AT THE PIANO, 1892

In 1892 the poet Stéphane Mallarmé and the art critic Claude Roger-Marx persuaded Henri Roujon, the Director of the Beaux-Arts, to purchase a Renoir painting for the State collection. An informal commission resulted in Renoir painting five versions of *Young Girls at the Piano*. The state purchased one of the pictures on 2 May 1892 for the sum of 4,000 francs. The State had only acquired paintings by one other of the original Impressionist group, Alfred Sisley. Mallarmé stated his support for Renoir in a letter to Roujon: *'It is my feeling, as well as the agreed opinion of everyone else, that you cannot be sufficiently congratulated on having chosen such a definitive, refreshing, bold work of maturity for a museum.'*
Two years earlier Renoir's friends had asked on his behalf to be decorated by the State for his work as a painter, but Renoir refused the honour.

NEWS OF THE DIFFERENT EXHIBITIONS

There is an exhibition of the INTRANSIGENTS (Impressionists) in the Boulevard des Capucines, or rather, you might say, of the LUNATICS, of which I have already given you a report. If you would like to be amused, and have a little time to spare, don't miss it.

At the time of the first Impressionist exhibitions the press were very hostile. This article is from the paper *La Patrie* on 14th May 1874

A PERFECT DAY

The quintessential Renoir image is a summer's day, pretty girls, wholesome food and a relaxed country setting. This imagery and the values it represents for today's audience have been adopted by the advertising industry.

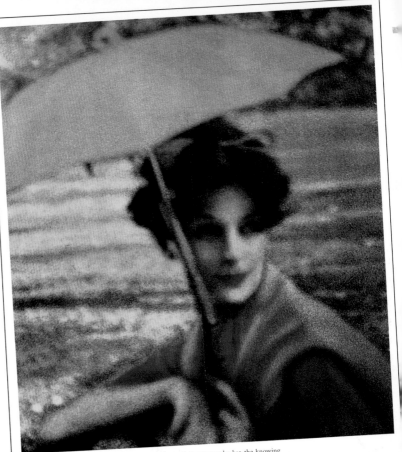

DURAND-RUEL

The art dealer Paul Durand-Ruel was influential in establishing Renoir's reputation. Durand-Ruel had been a long standing friend of Renoir and organized several solo exhibitions of his work, including a major retrospective of his work in 1892, and at his galleries in New York and the Grafton Galleries in London in 1905.

A LASTING IMPRESSION

*R*enoir died in 1919 at the age of seventy-eight. On the morning of his death he asked for paintbox and brushes despite being terribly ill with pneumonia. His son, Jean Renoir, wrote in his memoirs; *'He painted the anenomes which Nenette, our kind-hearted maid, had gone out and gathered for him. For several hours he identified himself with these flowers and forgot his pain. Then he motioned for someone to take his brush and said "I think I am beginning to understand something about it." He died in the night.'* Even before his death he had taken his place among the roll-call of great artists. His portrait of Madame Charpentier was acquired by the Louvre and he was fêted as his chair was wheeled through the galleries. His output was considerable; greater perhaps then any of his fellow Impressionist painters, having painted about 6,000 pictures. Today his works can be found in the major art galleries around the world, particularly in America because American collectors acquired his pictures when they were still unfashionable in Europe.

ALBERT BARNES

One of Renoir's greatest patrons was Albert Barnes, an American millionaire and art collector. Barnes created the Barnes Foundation in 1922, an educational foundation and museum containing many Impressionist paintings as well as those by artists such as Manet and Matisse. The Foundation owns 180 paintings by Renoir, as well as 69 by Cézanne and 60 by Matisse. Barnes believed that Renoir's art was richer than that of his Impressionist contemporaries because he built upon the Impressionist style to develop a more perceptive style of painting. The Barnes Foundation originally restricted access to its collection but now the works are made available for loan to exhibitions.

LES COLLETTES & RENOIR'S STUDIO

Since 1960 Renoir's house at Cagnes-sur-Mer, Les Collettes, has been preserved by the Renoir Estate and the local government as a museum. It is surrounded by its 100-year-old olive grove and is a place of pilgrimage for Renoir students. Several works by

the artist are still at Les Collettes. Another location which has been preserved in memory of the artist is the Fournaise Restaurant on Chatou island in the Seine, known locally as the Impressionist's island. It is possible today to have lunch on the same terrace made famous in Renoir's masterpiece *Luncheon of the Boating Party*.

GLOSSARY

Porcelain - A ceramic material which is renowned for its translucent qualities and mainly used for manufacturing vases, cups and plates. It is made from kaolin (a type of clay) and a paste that includes substances such as soapstone and bone ash. The finished product is of fine quality and lends itself to decoration. Renoir started his career painting images on porcelain.

Rococo - This word derives form the French word *rocaille* (rock work) and is applied to a decorative style which became prominent in the early 18th century. France and Southern Germany are best known for architecture, painting and decorative arts which were made in the rococo style and which is exemplified by small curves, rounded forms and sometimes excessive ornamentation.

Gustave Courbet (1819-77) - An extremely influential artist who was largely self-taught and whose art was based on the rejection of idealization and Romanticism in favour of realism which he believed was truly democratic and 'noble'. His depictions of peasants working in the fields and stone quarries were largely unpopular but his work was admired by the new generation of Impressionists who valued his rejection of the classical in favour of his depiction of the real world around him.

Louvre - The most famous national museum and art gallery in France. Originally a Parisian royal palace built around 1546, it has been a venue for displaying art since 1793 and today attracts more visitors than any other museum or gallery in France.

Bas-relief - Relief is sculpture which is not free-standing but is similar to a painting with raised surfaces. The depth of the projections from the background determines the name given to a relief, normally cast in bronze or built up in plaster, clay or a similar material. High-relief (*alto-relievo*) has very deep projections compared with bas-relief (*basso-relievo*).

Belle époque - A French term to describe the period of life in the late 19th century and early 20th century up to the First World War. The belle époque (translated as 'fine period') was notable for its comfortable lifestyle free from major conflicts.

ACKNOWLEDGEMENTS

We would like to thank: Graham Rich and Elizabeth Wiggans for their assistance.
Copyright © 1998 ticktock Publishing Ltd.
First published in Great Britain by ticktock Publishing Ltd.,
The Offices in the Square, Hadlow, Tonbridge, Kent, TN11 0DD. All rights reserved.
No part of this publication may be reproduced, stored in a retrieval system, or transmitted in any form or by any means electronic, mechanical, photocopying, recording or otherwise, without prior written permission of the copyright owner.

A CIP catalogue record for this book is available from the British Library. ISBN 1 86007 081 7
Picture research by Image Select.
Printed in Hong Kong.

Picture Credits: t=top, b=bottom, c=centre, l=left, r=right, OFC=outside front cover, IFC=inside front cover, IBC=inside back cover, OBC=outside back cover.

The Advertising Archives; 30tr. Archive Durand-Ruel; 25/25cb, 30bl. The Barnes Foundation; 31tr. Bridgeman Art Library; OFC (main pic), 8/9t, 15cr, 19bl, 20bl & 20tr, 23t, 25tl, 26l. Giraudon; 2/3t, 4tl, 4bl 4/5t, 6/7t & OFC, 6/7b, 7l, 8bl, 9cl & 9br, 10cb, 10/11t, 10/11b, 11tr & OBC, 12bl & OBC, 12/13t, 13cl, 13br, 14bl & 14/15t & 14/15cb& 15tr & IFC, 16bl, 16tl & 16/17t & 17cb & 17bl & 17br & 32ct, 18l & 18/19t & 19br, 20/2c 21tl, 21r, 22tl, 23bl, 24bl, 24tr, 26/27c, 27tr, 27bl & 27br, 28tl, 28/29cb, 29tr, 30br. Mairie de Paris © Photothèque des Musées de la Ville de Paris; 2bl. National Gallery of Washington; 4/5b. Réunion des Musée Nationaux © Photo RMN-Gérard Blot; 22/23cb. Union Centrale des Arts Decortifs; 3r.

Every effort has been made to trace the copyright holders and we apologise in advance for any unintentional omissions. We would be pleased to insert the appropriate acknowledgement in any subsequent edition of this publication.

snapping-turtle guide